DAILY MUSINGS

CHHAVI GARG

DEDICATION

This book is Dedicated to school-going Children in grades four to six.

I hope they will enjoy reading my creations.

Contents

Foreword

This is my first attempt to write a Poetry Book for Childrern.

The poems in this book take inspiration from nature and from things we see in our everyday lives.

It may make you laugh, make you cry , set you thinking or take you down the memory lane.

I have tried to take the young readers along with me, to expand their imagination,

and to feel as if the events are happening right before their eyes.

Acknowledgements

I am thankful to my Family, my husband (Gopesh Garg), and my sister (Shruti Gupta - she was the one to remind me of my writing talent,& encouraged me to start writing again). I used to write short stories when I was in school, but I never got the courage to get them published in the School Magazine.

My mother (Dr. Shailesh Maheshwari) and my dear friends for continuously encouraging me to write.

They all were a source of inspiration, who believed in me and encouraged me to write.

Prologue

PROLOGUE

The poems in this book take inspiration from everyday life, and from nature.

Poems in this book take you to different situations or happenings of everyday life.

Some poems take the readers into the midst of nature, making them feel happy and in tranquility at the same time.

1. WINDS IN THE MOUNTAINS

Winds in the mountains,
Like a song in the fountain,
Hustling and rustling
Through every flower
and tree,
Makes every heart full
With glee,
Winds in the mountains,
Like a song in the fountain,
Passing through every waterfall, river, or stream,
Is a place that is everyone's dream,
Winds in the mountains,
Like a song in the fountain,
It makes us complete and whole,
As it soothes our soul.

2. WATERFALLS

Tall and serene waterfalls,
Sun shining bright in overalls,
Quenching the thirst of all whether
A bird, bear, or bumblebee,
Meandering through the mountains,
Shining like a silver serpent,
Quenching the thirst of all whether
Woods, step fields, people or trees,
Tall and serene waterfalls,
Sun shining bright in overalls,
Meeting the river is certain,
The sea is its final destination.

3. ANTS ON MY WINDOW

Ants on my window,
Running in a row,
Carrying different food,
To feed their troops,

Ants on my window,
Running in a row,
Following one another,
Taking their injured brother

Ants on my window,
Running in a row,
Gathering all grass and leaves,
To save their colony
from the strong breeze.

4. HOT AIR BALLOON

There goes a hot air balloon,
It flies over a blue lagoon,
It takes you from place to place,
It shows you mountains and valleys
That amaze,

It shows you the charming sunrise,
It shows you the shimmering moonlight,
It shows you beautiful lands and meadows,
Where musical sounds of birds, bees, and deer echos,

It shows you far-off places,
Of which you dream,
There goes a hot air balloon,
It flies over a blue lagoon.

5. LIFE IN THE GARDEN

Life in the garden
Is full of fun,
Here we get joys by the ton,
There runs a chameleon
Under the bright sun,
Look at the shinning web the
Spider has spun,

There are flowers in all hues and shades,
There are bushes and shrubs
Of colour of jade,
There are grass hoppers and ladybugs
Under the shade,
See how beautiful is the nest,
The tailor bird has made,

There goes a chipmunk,
Scurrying here and there,
Gathering nuts and seeds,
Before the winter's here,

Life in the garden,
Is full of fun,
Face of the garden changes,
With every season.

6. THE FOOT BRIDGE

The solid, strong and sturdy foot bridge,
Leading to a spectacular ridge,
It stands tall and majestic,
Though looks frail and rustic,

Charming flowers
Adorning its path,
Leading the way
to the leafy footpath,

The leafy footpath takes us
To a place,
Where flowers on the hills are
Dancing with grace,

The foot bridge leads to
Many beautiful mysteries,
Leading to the woods,
Where animals, birds, bees,
butterflies and fireflies live in bliss.

7. PINE TREES

Tall, dark and high pine trees,
Standing high, as if touching the sky,
It's head up amongst the clouds,
Shining bright are the pine cones
Up on the pine tree,

Some are long, some are oval,
Some are woody,
Others are tan coloured, conical,
Cylindrical or scaly,

The trees shed the pine cones
Sometimes daily or sometimes rarely,
Swaying its head with the breeze,
Their heads covered with snow,
All their needles glow,

Glittering upon the pine trees,
Snow is all around as far as one can see,
Some are bright green, others are tall,
Dark and uncanny,
Many of them look old as my granny,

CHHAVI GARG

Some are as young as a manny,

Different in shapes and size,
But standing tall side by side,
They have all the flora and fauna beside,
Sharp, sweet and refreshing,

As the wiff of fresh air,
Is the fragrance of pine trees.

8. CUCKOO UPON THE MANGO TREE

Cuckoo upon the mango tree,
Announces the mango season
For free,

Singing in the shade of the mango
Tree,
Feeling its cool breeze,
Accompanying the cuckoo are the birds
And monkeys,
Seeing all the fruit
Makes them hungry,

They all want to
Taste the mangoes
As sweet as honey,
But some are sweet
While others are tart,

Cuckoo upon the mango tree,
Announces the mango season for free,

CHHAVI GARG

All make haste while the
Mango season lasts,
Cherishing its memories,
Long after the season has passed.

9. NATURE'S BOUNTY

All cheer the nature's bounty,
They all are flourishing in
the county,

Flowers, gardens or fresh
Produce,
There are oranges, strawberries and
Blueberries to juice,

Spinach, fenugreek, amaranth
and mustard greens,
All are full of micronutrients,

All cheer the nature's bounty,
They all are flourishing in
the county,

Squash, pumpkin, turnips, tomatoes,
Carrots and beets,
Fresh in the soup,

CHHAVI GARG

Meet all our needs,

Hazelnuts, cashew nuts, apricots,
Walnuts and pine nuts,
Keep us warm and strong,
Through the winter days,

Melons, mangoes, mulberries,
Papaya or pear make our day,
Refreshing as a cut fruit,
Smoothie or shake,

We receive nature's blessings,
Through these ways.

10. NEEM TREE

Majestic, huge, evergreen Neem tree,
It gives all beings
Fresh, cool, clean air for free,

Children play in its shade,
It's leaves shine in sunlight
Like jade,

In its lap are the abode
Of sparrows, parrots and crows,
All living together on the Neem tree,
Weather friend or foe,

It's flowers are white,
From which a pleasant fragrance arise,
It's branches reaching up the skies,
It's fruit is bitter,
But it makes our health better,

It's leaves are used for its medicinal property,
It's uses are plenty,
It's twig is used to clean our teeth,

CHHAVI GARG

It meets all our oral needs,

It's bark is used to treat various diseases,
Due to which the visits
To the doctor ceases,

All the parts of the Neem tree,
Are beneficial for humanity.

11. MOONLIGHT

Sparkling, shining, shimmering moonlight,
It's shine make the sky bright,
Changing its face every day,
It soothes the heart after a hard day,

It's light sparkles not only
The night sky,
It brightens the roads,
Trees, rivers, fields or hay,
It brightens whatever comes on its way,

Children play under its shadow,
Making figures in the meadow,
Children's laughter make an echo,
It's musical sound brightens
Up the lonely meadow,

It brightens everyone's heart,
Just like the flowers in the
Garden cart.

12. RAINY DAY

All welcome the rainy day,
After the hot summer of May,
There are clouds all over the Blue skies,
It's a delightful scene for the eyes,

All welcome the rainy day,
Whether woods, rivers, or lakes,
There's rain on the window pane,
Making a sweet sound
Like a musical wave,

All welcome the rainy day,
Whether young, old or
Middle-aged,

There's rain on the
Buildings, houses, and trees,
All shining bright
After a quick shower,
Dried with a breeze,

It brings laughter and cheer

To the children's faces,
As the puddles of water
Amazes,

All welcome the rainy day,
With the promise of
The rainbow is on the way.

13. SEA

The waves on the sea,
are calling us with glee,
They are sometimes gentle,
sometimes wild,
at times dark and huge,
that no one can guarantee,

Waves on the sea are
glittering and shining,
like silver in the sunlight,
All friends agree,

We take our boat out on
the sea waves,
riding the waves
without a fee,

There are ships and sailors,
cargos and containers,
passenger and adventurer,
They are all the tamers of the sea.

14. THE CLOCK

Tick tock, tick tock,
runs the hands of
the clock,
One is big, another is
small,
But they run
nonstop,

Tick tock, tick tock,
runs the hands of the clock,
Changing hours,
minutes and seconds,
reminding us of the changing season,

Tick tock, tick tock,
runs the hands of the clock,
changing a layman
into a legend,

Tick tock, tick tock,
runs the hands of the clock,
turning sorrow into

happiness tomorrow,

Tick tock, tick tock,
runs the hands of the clock,
children follow
the song of the chirping sparrow,

Tick tock, tick tock
runs the hands of the clock,
reminding us to find joy in all
moments,
As moments become memories,
with changing months, years, and centuries,

Tick tock, tick tock,
runs the hands of the clock.

15. BUTTERFLIES

Beautiful delicate butterflies,
Traveling miles and miles,
Hopping from one flower to another,
Drinking all the delicious nectar,

Beautiful delicate butterflies,
Flying far and near,
Mingling with one another,
Having the delicious nectar,
for breakfast, lunch, and supper,

Swift beautiful butterflies,
Charming our hearts
With their bright colors,

Exquisite elegant butterflies,
Dancing with the winds,
Fluttering their dainty wings,

Angelic shining butterflies,
Skipping here and there,
Traveling all the miles

CHHAVI GARG

Without a fare,

It gives us a sign
From the divine,
That everything will be fine.

16. FREEDOM

We celebrate our freedom
Honouring our freedom fighters
Wisdom,

They led our way,
Showing us a bright ray,
Our freedom is close to our bosom,
It increases our life's spectrum,

All the Indian citizens,
Had a common mission,
They were brave,
For their lives they gave,

Celebration of freedom,
Is a memorable tradition.

17. ROAD TRIP

We went on a road trip,
The baby cried as
We left his crib,

The twins broke into
A jig at the start
Of the road trip,

We crossed many paths,
One of them led
To the beautiful
Birdbath,

The road trip
was full of fun
And adventure,
It was a pleasant venture,

We came across different people
On the road,
Whether a hawker, shopper
Or a pauper,

We saw many people on the road,
Whose smile made our hearts glow,

We encountered many surprises,
We reached a place where sunrises,
It made our hearts sway,
Seeing the sun's first rays,

The children smiled with glee,
As I agreed to their plea,
They climbed on the mango tree,
On the roadside for free,

This is how we ended our road trip.
Full of happiness and adventure,
Bringing a smile to our hearts,
That I can confess.

18. KINGFISHER

Blue-breasted curious kingfisher
Hopping near the flowing river,
Shining colours of
White, green and blue,
Hopping happily in the dew,

Blue belted ringed kingfisher,
Catching its prey,
Resting in sunlight,
Near the bay,

Common pied happy kingfisher,
Feasting its heart filled,
Near the flowing river,
Feasting on fish, frogs, spiders, or crabs,
Filling its abs with delectable prey,

Moving swiftly and sprightly,
In and around the river,
Taking rest, in its nest,
It's sleep being addressed.

19. IN THE COUNTRYSIDE

In the countryside,
It's a beautiful day,
The hen laid its eggs
In a stack of hay
In the hot summers of May,

Mother chides her kids,
For the Toys they hid,
In the midst of the bundle of paddy,
To keep them safe from Tabby,

There are houses and farms,
fields and barns,
Kids play in the muddy puddle,
With a lamb in their arms,

Plough, rake, spade, sickle,
bullock cart and hoe,
Helps to tend to the crops
In each row,

CHHAVI GARG

Cattle in the shed are well-fed,
They follow the happy farmer,
To the meadow,
Where they are led,

The cattle and the poultry reside
Side by side,
In the countryside,
It's a beautiful sight!

20. SUNSHINE

Glittering, Shimmering sunshine,
Making everyone's heart shine,
Sparkling trees, bushes and all greens,

Shimmering, shining and sparkling river,
Glowing, glistening, gushing river,
Fishes,turtles, toads, snails and worms,
Soaking themselves in the beautiful sunshine
Turn by turn,
Some days its soft, some days its stern,

Bright, brilliant, dazzling sunshine,
passing through the dense forest,
Reaching all plants and trees
Even which are farthest,

Bright, dazzling, shining sunshine,
Making everything dazzle
Just like a gem brand new,
Whether honey, rain drop or dew.

21. ZOO

A visit to the zoo,
A cool refreshing
Breeze blew,

The children squealed with joy,
At the sight of a chimpanzee,
Who looked like a wild pansy,

They saw the proud Lion,
It looked bold and majestic,
The children were fearful of its roar,
But with it, their excitement soared,

Next, they visited the elephant,
It was wise, gentle, curious, and playful,
It took the children's caps,
But it returned their caps in a snap,
The kids were grateful to the angelic chap,

They moved further
To different cages,
Next, they saw the chirpy parrots,

They were all of different ages,
They squealed with delight,
As the parrots were a great mimic,
Along with being a great athlete,

After meeting the members
of the animal kingdom,
They all made a beautiful memory
in the children's photo album.